Cambridge Primary

CW00486075

Hodder Cambridge Primary
Maths
Workbook

Stage 4

Josh Lury

Series editors: Mike Askew and Paul Broadbent

HODDER
EDUCATION
AN HACHETTE UK COMPANY

Acknowledgements

With warm thanks to Jennifer Peek for her help in shaping and developing this title.

The Publisher is extremely grateful to the following schools for their comments and feedback during the development of this series:
Avalon Heights World Private School, Ajman
The Oxford School, Dubai
Al Amana Private School, Sharjah
British International School, Ajman
Wesgreen International School, Sharjah
As Seeb International School, Al Khoud.

Practice test exam-style questions and sample answers are written by the author.

Every effort has been made to trace all copyright holders, but if any have been inadvertently overlooked the Publishers will be pleased to make the necessary arrangements at the first opportunity.

Although every effort has been made to ensure that website addresses are correct at time of going to press, Hodder Education cannot be held responsible for the content of any website mentioned in this book. It is sometimes possible to find a relocated web page by typing in the address of the home page for a website in the URL window of your browser.

Hachette UK's policy is to use papers that are natural, renewable and recyclable products and made from wood grown in sustainable forests. The logging and manufacturing processes are expected to conform to the environmental regulations of the country of origin.

Orders: please contact Bookpoint Ltd, 130 Milton Park, Abingdon, Oxon OX14 4SB. Telephone: (44) 01235 827720. Fax: (44) 01235 400454. Lines are open from 9.00–5.00, Monday to Saturday, with a 24-hour message answering service. You can also order through our website www.hoddereducation.com

© Josh Lury 2017

Published by Hodder Education

An Hachette UK Company

Carmelite House, 50 Victoria Embankment, London EC4Y 0DZ

Impression number	9
Year	2021

All rights reserved. Apart from any use permitted under UK copyright law, no part of this publication may be reproduced or transmitted in any form or by any means, electronic or mechanical, including photocopying and recording, or held within any information storage and retrieval system, without permission in writing from the publisher or under licence from the Copyright Licensing Agency Limited. Further details of such licences (for reprographic reproduction) may be obtained from the Copyright Licensing Agency Limited, Saffron House, 6–10 Kirby Street, London EC1N 8TS.

Cover illustration by Steve Evans

Illustrations by DTP Impresssions

Typeset in FS Albert 15/17 by DTP Impressions

Printed in Great Britain by Ashford Colour Press Ltd.

A catalogue record for this title is available from the British Library

9781471884634

Contents

Unit 1 Number and problem solving

Can you remember?

Read these numbers and then write them as figures.

a One thousand, one hundred and twenty-three = ☐☐☐☐

b Four thousand, three hundred and twenty-one = ☐☐☐☐

c Four thousand and four = ☐☐☐☐

d Four thousand and forty = ☐☐☐☐

e Three thousand, three hundred and three = ☐☐☐☐

f Three thousand and thirty-three = ☐☐☐☐

Place value and decimals

1 Use only the digits 9 and 1 to complete each statement.

a ☐☐☐☐ is between 1 900 and 2 000.

b ☐☐☐☐ is between 1 100 and 1 120.

c ☐☐☐☐ is between 1 120 and 1 200.

d ☐☐☐☐ is between 9 000 and 9 200.

e ☐☐☐☐ is between 9 800 and 9 920.

f ☐☐☐☐ is between 9 900 and 9 990.

2 Use the counting rule to complete the counting patterns.

Starting number							End number	Counting rule
a	2 000							+1 000
b		2 000						+100
c			2 000					+10
d				2 000				−10
e					2 000			−100
f						2 000		−1 000

3 How many different numbers can you make using these digits?

5136 _____

_____

_____

Now, spin your own spinner four times. Use the digits to write at least ten of your own numbers.

_____

_____

1	3
5	6

I can make 5136 using these digits.

5

Comparing numbers

 1 Write the missing numbers.

a

b
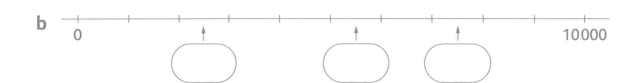

c
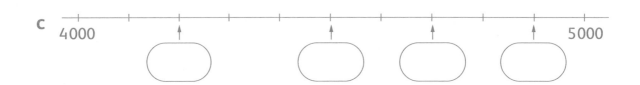

d
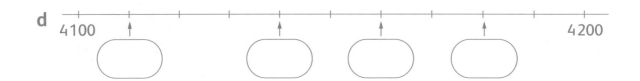

e

 **2** Complete by using the symbols **<** or **>**.

a 1234 ⬚ 1243

b 5010 ⬚ 6001

c 1324 ⬚ 1234

d 5110 ⬚ 4999

e 2100 ⬚ 2011

f 501 ⬚ 510

g 1010 ⬚ 1001

h 5099 ⬚ 999

i 2021 ⬚ 2220

j 5999 ⬚ 610

3

Use the four digits above to complete this inequality statement.

		>		

You can only use a digit once for each solution.

How many different solutions can you write using the same four digits above?

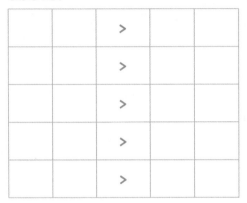 

4 I am thinking of a number. I double it. Now, when I round the answer to the nearest 10 it is 450, but when I round it to the nearest 100 it is 400. How many different possible starting numbers are there?

Addition and subtraction

 Decide if the estimate for each of these will be greater than (>) or less than (<) the exact answer.

Calculation	< or >	Estimate
21 + 61		20 + 60
121 + 161		120 + 160
29 + 59		30 + 60
229 + 259		230 + 260
33 + 73		30 + 70
333 + 473		330 + 470
65 + 75		70 + 80
165 + 275		170 + 280

2 Complete these number sentences by choosing +, − and =.

120 ⬭ 230 ⬭ 350   350 ⬭ 220 ⬭ 130

412 ⬭ 241 ⬭ 653   654 ⬭ 441 ⬭ 213

3 Find two different ways of completing these by using +, − and = signs.

a 420 ⬭ 105 ⬭ 315   **b** 770 ⬭ 660 ⬭ 110

  420 ⬭ 105 ⬭ 315   770 ⬭ 660 ⬭ 110

c 350 ⬭ 230 ⬭ 120   **d** 771 ⬭ 659 ⬭ 112

  350 ⬭ 230 ⬭ 120   771 ⬭ 659 ⬭ 112

4 Complete the number lines by writing the additions.
Then write an inverse subtraction for each one.

a

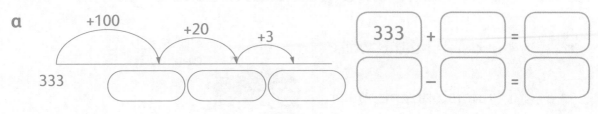

333 + [ ] = [ ]

[ ] − [ ] = [ ]

b

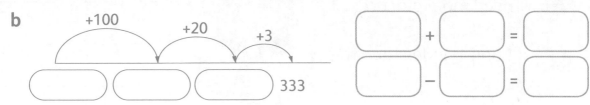

[ ] + [ ] = [ ]

[ ] − [ ] = [ ]

c

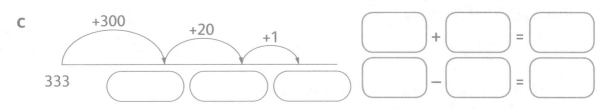

[ ] + [ ] = [ ]

[ ] − [ ] = [ ]

d

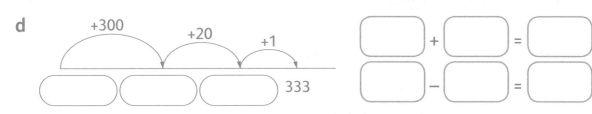

[ ] + [ ] = [ ]

[ ] − [ ] = [ ]

5 Play a game with your partner. Choose two numbers from the cloud.

11	22	33	44
111	222	333	444
55	555	66	666

Choose whether you want to add or subtract.

When you have worked out the answer, find the number in the grid. Cover it with a counter. If your answer is not in the grid, you miss a go.

The winner is the first person to get three in a row.

999	122	777	611
355	33	289	1 221
489	444	55	732
378	888	77	178

Self-assessment

Unit 1 Number and problem solving

😊 I understand this well.

😐 I understand this, but I need more practice.

☹ I don't understand this.

I need more help with ...

_____

_____

_____

Self-check statements	😊	😐	☹
I can read and write numerals representing numbers to ten thousand.			
I can count on and back in ones, tens, hundreds and thousands from numbers in the thousands.			
I can split numbers up to ten thousand into thousands, hundreds, tens and ones.			
I can round a three- or four-digit number to the nearest multiple of ten or one hundred.			
I can place numbers appropriately on a number line marked in 10s or 100s.			
I can estimate where to place numbers up to ten thousand on an empty number line.			
I can order numbers up to ten thousand and use the > and < signs appropriately.			
I can add a set of small numbers, looking for pairs that add to 10 or 20.			
I can add or subtract pairs of two-digit numbers mentally, or with a written method.			
I can use an appropriate method to add a pair of three-digit numbers.			
I can use an appropriate method to subtract a two- or three-digit number from a three-digit number.			

Unit 2 Measures and problem solving

Can you remember?

Fill in the missing numbers.

a $1000 + \boxed{} + 10 + \boxed{} = 1212$

b $\boxed{} + 200 + \boxed{} + \boxed{} + 3 = 1313$

c $4000 + \boxed{} + \boxed{} + \boxed{} + 2 = 5432$

d $\boxed{} + 300 + 40 + \boxed{} = 2345$

e $\boxed{} + \boxed{} + 20 + \boxed{} = 5135$

f $1000 + 500 + 50 + 1 = \boxed{}$

The metric system

1 Complete the missing information.

a $5\,m = \boxed{}\ cm$ b $5\,cm = \boxed{}\ mm$ c $8\,m = \boxed{}\ cm$

d $8\,cm = \boxed{}\ mm$ e $\boxed{}\ m = 900\,cm$ f $\boxed{}\ cm = 90\,mm$

g $\boxed{}\ cm = 900\,mm$

2 Measure each line to the nearest mm.

a ——— $= \boxed{}\ mm$ b $| = \boxed{}\ mm$

c ———— $= \boxed{}\ mm$ d $| = \boxed{}\ mm$

e —————— $= \boxed{}\ mm$

f ——————— $= \boxed{}\ mm$

g ———————— $= \boxed{}\ mm$

h ———————————— $= \boxed{}\ mm$

In a shed there are planks of wood of different lengths.
Sort them into four different groups so that each group has exactly 2 m of wood.

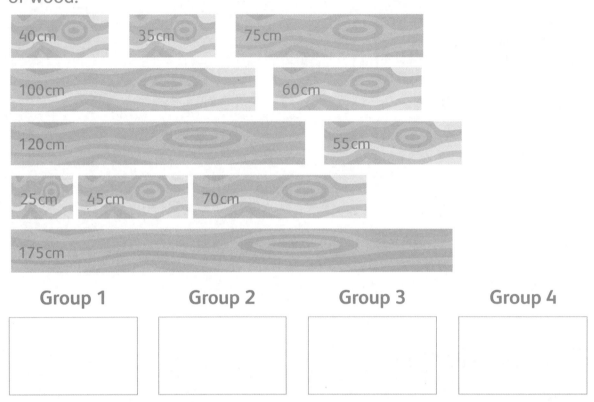

Group 1	Group 2	Group 3	Group 4

You can only travel along the grid lines. Draw a path that connects all the dots. Measure the total length of the journey.

Aim for the shortest journey. Compare your results with a partner.

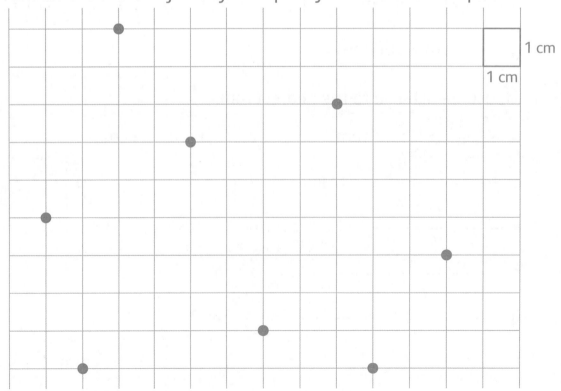

Length, area and perimeter

1 cm
1 cm

1 In each grid, draw a different rectangle, and write the perimeter in cm.

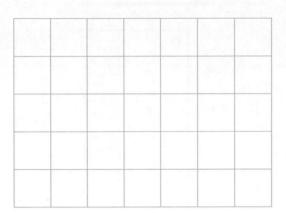

Perimeter = ⬚ cm

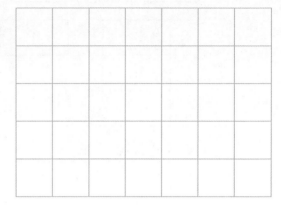

Perimeter = ⬚ cm

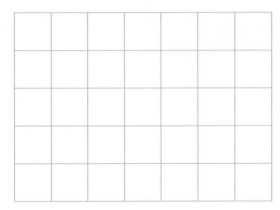

Perimeter = ⬚ cm

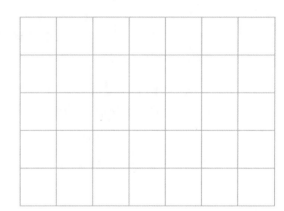

Perimeter = ⬚ cm

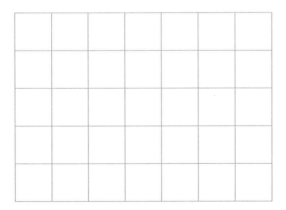

Perimeter = ⬚ cm

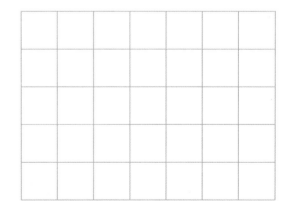

Perimeter = ⬚ cm

2 Sort these shapes into order, from shortest perimeter to longest.
Write the correct order of the letters.

_____, _____, _____, _____, _____, _____, _____.

3 Spin two 1–6 spinners. Multiply the scores.
Shade a shape that has the same area as the product of both spinners.
Take turns with a partner until the grid is too full to draw a shape with the area shown on the spinners.
If you cannot shade a shape with the area shown on the spinners, then you lose the game.

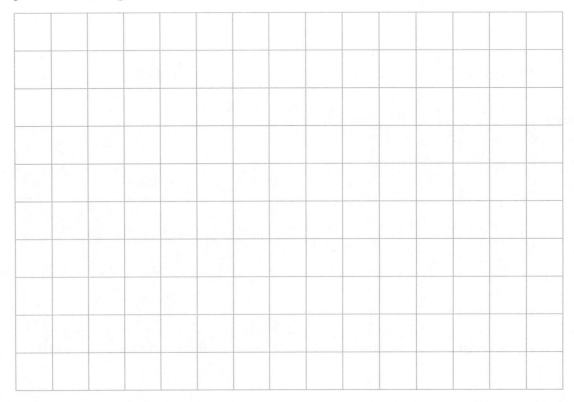

Time

 Draw the hands to show the time on each clock.

a 12.25  b 12.55  c 1.24  d 1.58

e 2.01  f 2.59  g 3.14  h 4.46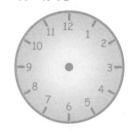

 Join the matching pairs.

2.15 p.m.	Half-past nine in the evening
9.30 a.m.	Quarter to three in the afternoon
3.15 p.m.	Quarter past three in the afternoon
9.30 p.m.	Quarter past two in the afternoon
2.15 a.m.	Quarter past two at night
2.45 p.m.	Half past nine in the morning

3 Write an estimate for how long each of these activities would usually take.

Brush teeth =  Walk to school =

Build a house = Mow the grass =

Read a book = Go on holiday =

4 Draw a likely activity for each time shown. Look closely for whether the time is a.m. or p.m.

a
a.m.
1:00

b
p.m.
1:00

c
a.m.
6:00

d
p.m.
6:00

e
a.m.
8:00

f
p.m.
8:00

Self-assessment

Unit 2 Measures and problem solving

😊 I understand this well.

😐 I understand this, but I need more practice.

☹ I don't understand this.

I need more help with …

_____

_____

_____

Self-check statements	😊	😐	☹
I can measure lengths, widths and heights in different units of measure and record my results.			
I can use and explain the relationship between the metric units for length.			
I can interpret and read measuring scales.			
I can draw rectangles, measure them and calculate their perimeters.			
I can use a square grid to find areas of simple shapes.			
I can tell the time to the nearest minute on both digital and analogue clocks.			
I can read and record times using a.m, p.m. and on a 12-hour digital clock.			
I can choose what might be the best unit to measure how long something takes.			
I can estimate answers to calculations and check my working.			
I can make up a story problem for a measurement calculation.			

Can you remember?

a 5 cm = [ ] mm   **b** [ ] mm = 8 cm   **c** 80 cm = [ ] mm

d [ ] cm = 130 mm   **e** 17 cm = [ ] mm

Number patterns

1 Use these numerals to complete the number sentences. (You can use each number more than once.)

27   35   50   70   44   36

a [ ] and [ ] are both multiples of 3.

b [ ] and [ ] and [ ] are multiples of 5.

c [ ] and [ ] are multiples of 2 and 5.

d [ ] and [ ] are both multiples of 4.

e [ ] and [ ] are not multiples of 2.

2 Use each multiple of five in the cloud once to complete the number sentences.

a [ ] + [ ] = a multiple of 10

b [ ] + [ ] = a multiple of 100.

c [ ] + [ ] + [ ] = a multiple of 10.

d [ ] + [ ] = a multiple of 5.

225, 230, 240, 270, 290, 300, 310 235, 250

I am thinking of a multiple of 5. I add 90 and now I have a multiple of 100.

I am thinking of a multiple of 5 and I subtract 90. Now I have a multiple of 100.

Think of five different numbers that Alec and Lia could have started with. Show your calculations here.

Numbers for Alec	Numbers for Lia

Look at this Venn diagram. Write a number to go in each section.

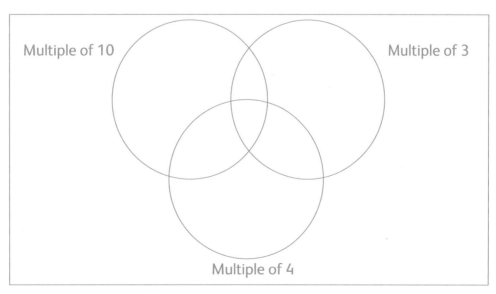

Discuss with a partner how this is the same or different from other Venn diagrams you have seen.

Multiplication and division

 Draw an array and complete each multiplication.

a 3 × 5 =

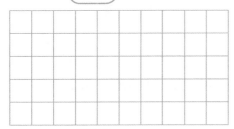

b 5 × 4 =

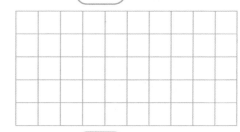

c 5 × 6 =

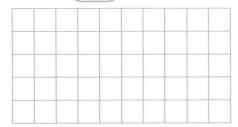

d 5 × 7 =

e 5 × 9 =

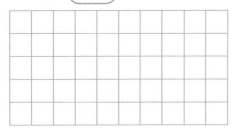

f 5 × 10 =

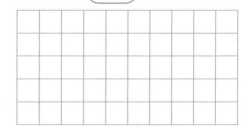

 Complete these patterns. The first one has been done for you.

a 2 × 4 = 8

    20 × 4 = 80

b 7 × 3 =

    70 × 3 =

c 3 × 3 = 9

    30 × 3 =

d 4 × 3 =

    40 × 3 =

e ⬜ × 5 = 35

    ⬜ × 5 = 350

f 6 × ⬜ = 12

    6 × ⬜ = 120

3 It costs $10 for each person to take a boat ride.
Complete the missing information in the table below.

Group size	Calculation	Total cost
8 people	☐ × $10	$ ☐
11 people	11 × $ ☐	$ ☐
15 people	☐ × ☐	$ ☐
☐ people	☐ × $10	$190
☐ people	23 × $10	$ ☐
☐ people	☐ × ☐	$330

4 Solve these. Think about the patterns you notice in the answers.

15 × 3 = _____   25 × 3 = _____   35 × 3 = _____

17 × 3 = _____   27 × 3 = _____   37 × 3 = _____

19 × 3 = _____   29 × 3 = _____   39 × 3 = _____

The patterns I noticed were _____

_____

_____

_____

_____

5 Write two division facts to go with each multiplication:

a 2 × 8 = 16

◻ ÷ ◻ = ◻

◻ ÷ ◻ = ◻

b 3 × 7 = 21

◻ ÷ ◻ = ◻

◻ ÷ ◻ = ◻

c 4 × 6 = 24

◻ ÷ ◻ = ◻

◻ ÷ ◻ = ◻

d 5 × 6 = ◻

◻ ÷ ◻ = ◻

◻ ÷ ◻ = ◻

e 3 × 4 = ◻

◻ ÷ ◻ = ◻

◻ ÷ ◻ = ◻

f 4 × 5 = ◻

◻ ÷ ◻ = ◻

◻ ÷ ◻ = ◻

6 How many solutions can you find for these multiplications?

◻ × ◻ = 25

◻ × ◻ = 25

◻ × ◻ = 25

◻ × ◻ = 25

◻ × ◻ = 25

◻ × ◻ = 25

◻ × ◻ = 25

◻ × ◻ = 24

◻ × ◻ = 24

◻ × ◻ = 24

◻ × ◻ = 24

◻ × ◻ = 24

◻ × ◻ = 24

◻ × ◻ = 24

Which column has the most solutions? _____

7 Write your own story problem about saving up for an item.

Work out how much you save each week, and how much it will cost to buy.

Make sure there are no remainders in your answer.

I save $3 a week. How long will it take me to save $42 to buy new trainers?

8 Play this game with a partner.

You will need: counters in two colours.

Put a counter in your colour on the grid over a number of your choice. Say a division that you think has that answer. Your partner must check it by using a multiplication.

If you are right, you keep your counter on the square. If you are wrong, your partner puts a counter on the square.

You cannot repeat any divisions. The winner is the first person to have four in a row.

9	3	4	10	5
5	10	4	3	9
9	3	4	10	5
5	10	4	3	9
9	3	4	10	5

I say 24 ÷ 4 = 4.

I have checked by using the inverse: 4 × 4 = 16, so you are incorrect. Sorry!

Self-assessment

Unit 3 Number and problem solving

😊 I understand this well.

😐 I understand this, but I need more practice.

🙁 I don't understand this.

I need more help with …

_____

_____

_____

Self-check statements	😊	😐	🙁
I can say whether a number up to 1000 is a multiple of 5, 10, or 100.			
I can say whether a number up to 50 is a multiple of 2, 3, 4, 5, or 10.			
I can explain what happens when a number up to 1000 is multiplied or divided by 10.			
I can use my knowledge of multiplying single digits to multiply multiples of ten by a single digit.			
I can explain why I think a mental or written method may be the best for a given calculation.			
I can multiply and divide two-digit numbers by a single digit.			
I can state a related division calculation for a given multiplication and vice versa.			
I can make up a story problem to go with a multiplication or division.			
I can estimate the answer to multiplication and division calculations.			
I can predict whether or not my estimates are greater or less than the actual answer.			
I can explain why I think my answer to a problem is likely to be correct.			

Unit 4 Geometry and problem solving

Can you remember?

a 10 × 2 = ☐

b 6 × 10 = ☐

c ☐ × 10 = 120

d 10 × ☐ = 240

e 20 × 3 = ☐

f ☐ × 5 = 150

Classifying shapes

1 Use this dotty paper to draw at least six different triangles.

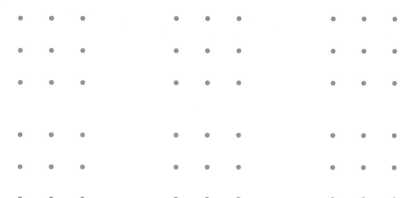

2 Design four different pentagons and four different hexagons.
Show any right angles by marking them with a coloured pencil.

Shade as many different shapes as you can on these diagrams. Write the name for each shape that you know. The first one has been done for you.

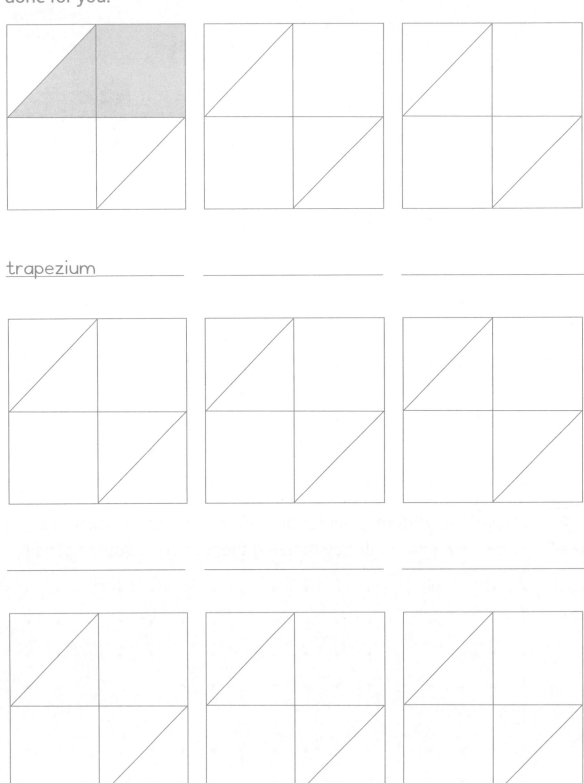

trapezium

2-D shapes

 Complete these symmetrical shapes. The dotted line is a mirror line.

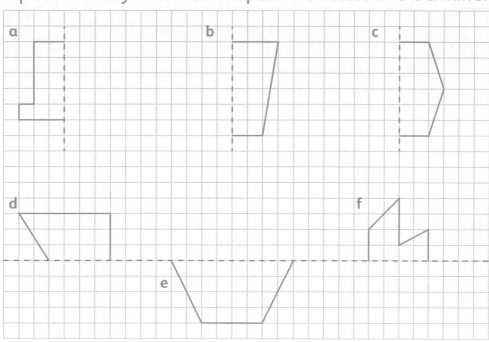

 a Draw four different symmetrical triangles.

b Draw four different symmetrical four-sided shapes (quadrilaterals).

c Draw four different shapes that have both horizontal and vertical symmetry. Show the mirror lines for each drawing.

3 Investigate which letters of the alphabet have symmetry. Draw mirror lines on any letters that have symmetry.

A   B   C   D   E   F   G   H   I

J   K   L   M   N   O   P   Q   R

S   T   U   V   W   X   Y   Z

Write the letters in the correct column in the table according to what symmetry they have. Some letters may go in two places.

Letters with horizontal symmetry	Letters with vertical symmetry	Letters with no symmetry

4 Write a message using your symmetrical letters. Draw half of each letter, ready for your partner to complete the other half.

Switch messages with your partner, and see who can crack the code first!

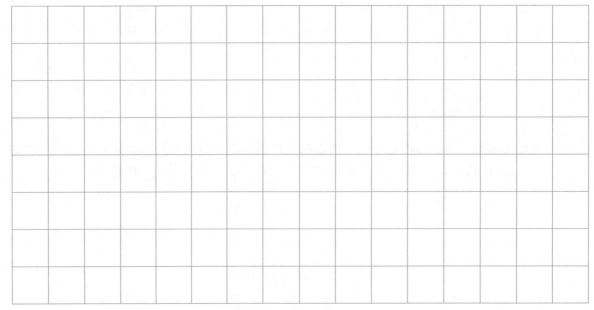

Position and movement

 Shade the squares given by these grid references.

Grid a: A1, B2, C3, D4, E5, A5, B4, D2, E1

Grid b: A3, C1, B3, C2, C3, D3, C4, E3, C5

a

5					
4					
3					
2					
1					
	A	B	C	D	E

b

5					
4					
3					
2					
1					
	A	B	C	D	E

Grid c: B2, D4, C2, C4, D2, B4, D3, B3

Grid d: B1, D1, B5, D5, B3, D3, A2, A4, E2, E4, C2, C4

c

5					
4					
3					
2					
1					
	A	B	C	D	E

d

5					
4					
3					
2					
1					
	A	B	C	D	E

 These are two corners of a square. Where are the last two corners?

5					
4			•		
3					
2			•		
1					
	A	B	C	D	E

5					
4			•		
3					
2			•		
1					
	A	B	C	D	E

5					
4			•		
3					
2			•		
1					
	A	B	C	D	E

There are three different solutions to this problem.
Draw circles for the other corners and shade the finished squares.

Draw your own map on this grid.

Include interesting features at these grid references: A5, C2, E8, H1, J10.

Key

 Try this!

Draw four dots for the corners of a rectangle on the grid.

Then draw the dots for another two rectangles in the same way.

Challenge your partner to find the grid references of all three rectangles.

Rectangle 1 = ⬚⬚ , ⬚⬚ , ⬚⬚ , ⬚⬚

Rectangle 2 = ⬚⬚ , ⬚⬚ , ⬚⬚ , ⬚⬚

Rectangle 3 = ⬚⬚ , ⬚⬚ , ⬚⬚ , ⬚⬚

Self-assessment

Unit 4 Geometry and problem solving

😃 I understand this well.

😐 I understand this, but I need more practice.

🙁 I don't understand this.

I need more help with …

_____

_____

_____

Self-check statements	😃	😐	🙁
I can name, describe and draw 2-D and 3-D shapes.			
I can sort a collection of polygons in several different ways according to their properties.			
I can find and sketch lines of symmetry in 2-D shapes and patterns.			
I can identify shapes and symmetry in drawings and around me.			
I can use a square grid to identify the position of things.			
I know that a right angle, quarter turn or 90° are equivalent and work with these.			
I can describe how 2-D and 3-D shapes are the same and how they are different.			
I can explore statements and come to a decision about whether they are true or not.			

Unit 6 Number and problem solving

Can you remember?

a ☐ + 25 = 100   b 65 + ☐ = 100   c 64 + ☐ = 100

d 100 = 10 + ☐   e 100 = ☐ + 89   f 100 − ☐ = 91

Numbers and the number system

 1 Round each number to the nearest 100 and to the nearest 10.

Number	Rounded to the nearest 100	Rounded to the nearest 10
91		
99		
591		
599		
5 678		
5 555		
5 591		
5 995		
5 999		

2 Write the correct temperatures for each place in the table below.

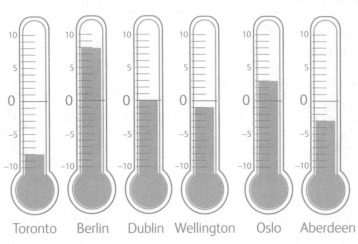

Toronto   Berlin   Dublin   Wellington   Oslo   Aberdeen

Place	Temperature in degrees
Toronto	
Berlin	
Dublin	
Wellington	
Oslo	
Aberdeen	

3 Convert mm and cm.

20 mm = ☐ cm   40 mm = ☐ cm   ☐ mm = 8 cm

☐ mm = 10 cm   21 mm = ☐ cm   41 mm = ☐ cm

☐ mm = 8.1 cm   ☐ mm = 10.1 cm   61 mm = ☐ cm

200 mm = ☐ cm   ☐ mm = 18.1 cm   ☐ mm = 108.1 cm

4 The grid is a 5 mm grid.

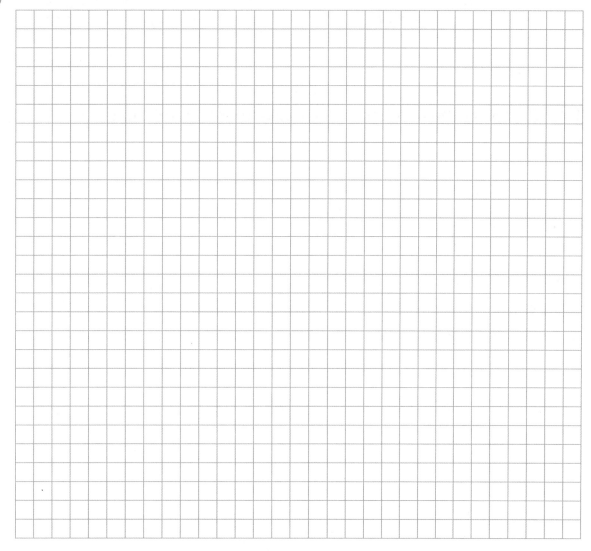

Draw the following rectangles. (The length is given first, then the width.)
Rectangle A – 25 mm by 40 mm   Rectangle D – 6.5 mm by 5 mm
Rectangle B – 3.5 cm by 1.5 cm   Rectangle E – 40 mm by 4.5 cm
Rectangle C – 10 mm by 5.5 cm   Rectangle F – 3.5 cm by 40 mm

Addition and subtraction

1 Find pairs of numbers that total 1000.

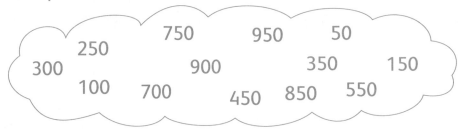

750	950	50
250		350	150
300	900		
100	700	450	850	550

◻ + ◻ = 1000   ◻ + ◻ = 1000

◻ + ◻ = 1000   ◻ + ◻ = 1000

◻ + ◻ = 1000   ◻ + ◻ = 1000

2 Complete the number lines to solve these subtractions.

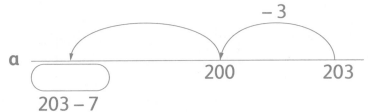

a   − 3
          200   203
203 − 7

b
          300   302
302 − 7

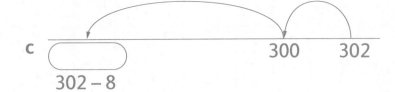

c
          300   302
302 − 8

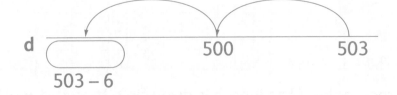

d
          500   503
503 − 6

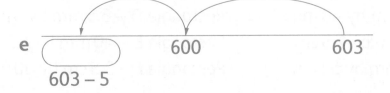

e
          600   603
603 − 5

3 Spin a 1–6 spinner and use the score to fill in a digit in one of the subtractions below. Repeat it to complete the subtraction.

Your aim is to have as many subtractions that give an answer ending in '9' as possible.

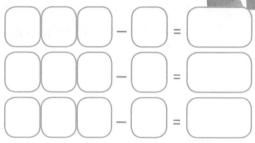

102 – 3 = 99. This subtraction ends in a '9'.

⬚⬚⬚ – ⬚ = ⬚   ⬚⬚⬚ – ⬚ = ⬚

⬚⬚⬚ – ⬚ = ⬚   ⬚⬚⬚ – ⬚ = ⬚

⬚⬚⬚ – ⬚ = ⬚   ⬚⬚⬚ – ⬚ = ⬚

Compare your scores with your partner. Who has the most answers that

end in a '9'? _____

4 Write each calculation in the correct column of the table.

20 + 81
20 + 79
22 + 79
41 + 61
130 + 71
31 + 160
41 + 150
41 + 160
42 + 159

Answer less than 100	Answer between 100 and 200	Answer greater than 200

5 Complete each subtraction using a number line, then write a fourth subtraction that follows the pattern.

a 241 – 23

b 352 – 34

c 442 – 45

d ⬚

6 This grid gives you 2 three-digit numbers to add together.

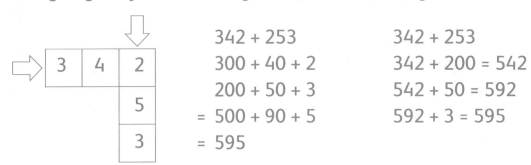

342 + 253

300 + 40 + 2

200 + 50 + 3

= 500 + 90 + 5

= 595

342 + 253

342 + 200 = 542

542 + 50 = 592

592 + 3 = 595

Make six different additions by rearranging the digits 2, 3, 3, 4 and 5.
Which method will you use to find the total?

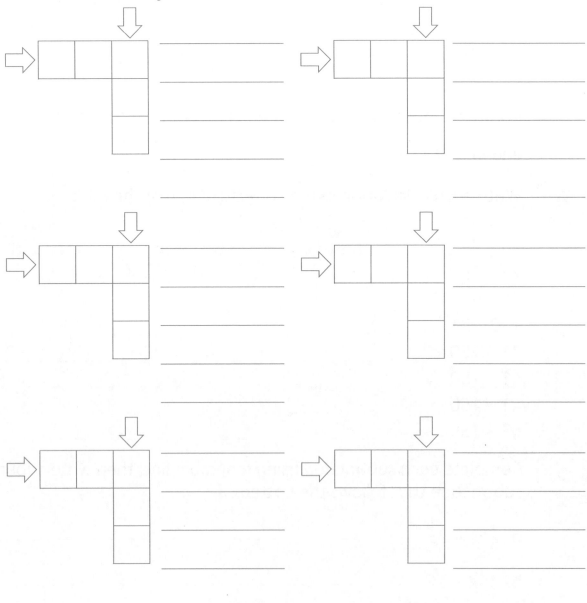

Write your answers in order, from the smallest to the largest number.

_____, _____, _____, _____, _____, _____

Self-assessment

Unit 6 Number and problem solving

😀 I understand this well.

😐 I understand this, but I need more practice.

☹ I don't understand this.

I need more help with …

_____

_____

_____

Self-check statements	😀	😐	☹
I can count on and back in ones, tens, hundreds and thousands from numbers in the thousands.			
I can split numbers up to one hundred thousand into thousands, hundreds, tens and units.			
I can record money and measures using decimal notation.			
I can read and interpret negative numbers on a thermometer.			
I can say whether a three- or four-digit number rounds up or down to the nearest multiple of ten.			
I can round a three- or four-digit number to the nearest multiple of ten.			
I can use an appropriate method to add a pair of three-digit numbers.			
I can use an appropriate method to subtract a two-digit number from a three-digit number.			
I can use an appropriate method to subtract a three-digit number from a three-digit number.			

Can you remember?

Fill in the missing lengths.

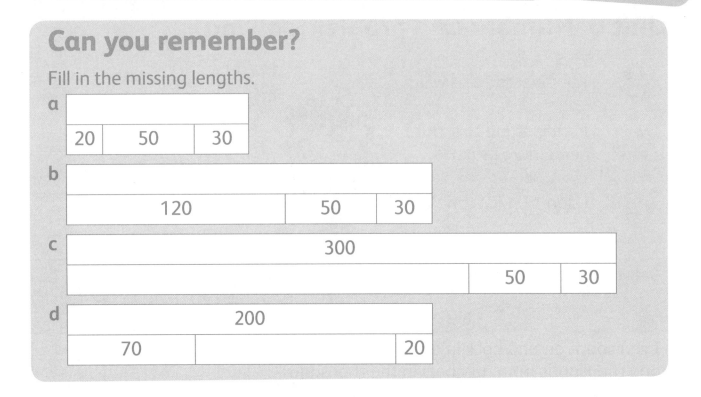

a

20	50	30

b

120	50	30

c

300		
	50	30

d

200		
70		20

The metric system

1 Draw arrows on the scale for each weight.

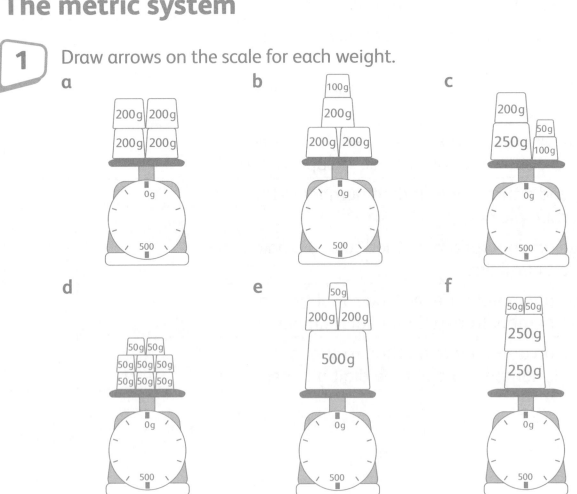

2 Complete the missing information:

[   ] g = 2 kg + 500 g   [   ] g = 4 kg + 250 g

3 500 g = [   ] kg + [   ] g   5 250 g = [   ] kg + [   ] g

1 200 g = [   ] kg + [   ] g + 50 g   1 750 g = [   ] kg + $\frac{1}{2}$ kg + [   ] g

3 250 g + [   ] g = 4 kg + 250 g   4 500 g + 3$\frac{1}{2}$ kg = [   ] kg

3 Arrange all the weights so that the scales balance.

a

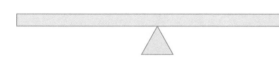

250g   1kg   100g
50g
$\frac{1}{2}$ kg   2kg   100g

b

200g   200g
100g
$\frac{1}{2}$ kg   1kg   200g

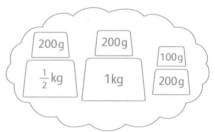

c

50g
250g
100g   1kg
500g
200g
1kg

4 Choose six different objects. List them below. Estimate which have a mass more or less than 2000 g. Then check using scales.

Less than 2 000 g	Actual mass	2 000 g or more	Actual mass

Length, area and perimeter

 Complete these rectangles and give the perimeter in millimetres:

a 2 cm and 3 cm

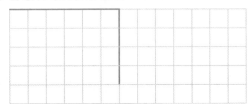

Perimeter of **a** = ☐ mm

b 2.5 cm and 3.5 cm

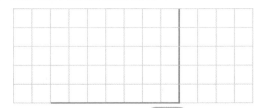

Perimeter of **b** = ☐ mm

c 4 cm and 2.5 cm

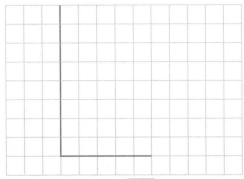

Perimeter of **c** = ☐ mm

d 4.5 cm and 5.5 cm

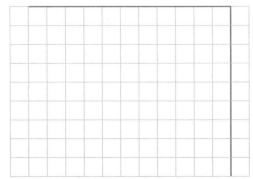

Perimeter of **d** = ☐ mm

e 9.5 cm and 1.5 cm

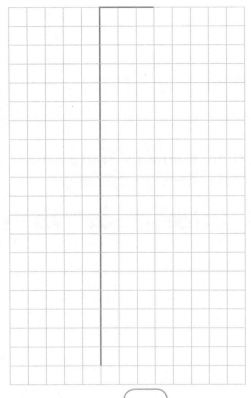

Perimeter of **e** = ☐ mm

f 10 cm and 1 cm

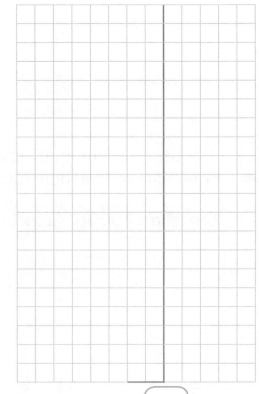

Perimeter of **f** = ☐ mm

2 Draw two or more different rectangles with the same area as the square.

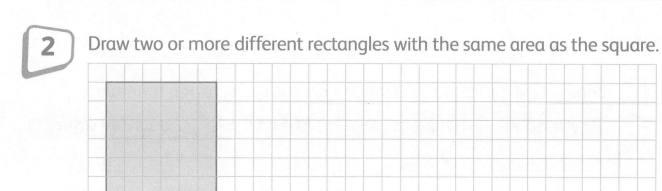

3 Draw two or more rectangles with the same perimeter as this shape.

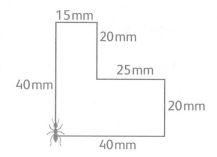

4 Draw a shape that has the same area as shape A and the same perimeter as shape B.

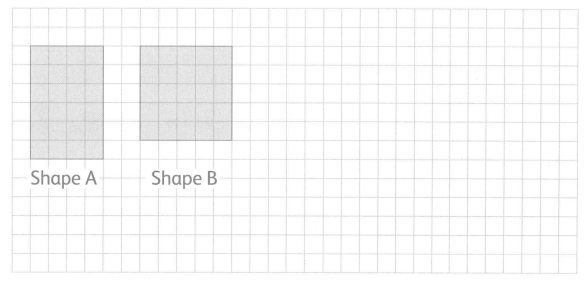

Shape A   Shape B

Time

 1 Complete the missing information on this train station timetable.

Destination	Departs	Arrives	Journey time
Forest Town	11 a.m.	2 p.m.	☐ hours
Rocketville	6.15 a.m.		4 hours
Lakeside		7.45 a.m.	5 hours
Treetops	8.30 p.m.		$2\frac{1}{2}$ hours
Bayside		8.30 p.m.	12 hours
Tiny Town		1.25 a.m.	11 hours

2 Look at the clocks on the station wall.
Use these number lines to work out how
long until each train departs.

a

Time on the clock   The train to Forest Town departs at 11 a.m.

The train will depart in _____ hours.

b

Time on the clock   The train to Rocketville departs at 6.15 a.m.

The train will depart in _____ hours and _____ minutes.

c

Time on the clock   The train to Treetops departs at 8.30 p.m.

The train will depart in _____.

d

Time on the clock   The train to Bayside departs at _____

The train will depart in _____.

Self-assessment

Unit 7 Measures and problem solving

😊 I understand this well.

😐 I understand this, but I need more practice.

☹️ I don't understand this.

I need more help with …

_____

_____

_____

Self-check statements	😊	😐	☹️
I can use and explain the relationship between the metric units for mass.			
I can interpret and read measuring scales.			
I can draw rectangles and measure and calculate their perimeters.			
I can use squares to find the areas of shapes.			
I can use decimals to estimate, measure and record lengths.			
I can read and record times using a.m., p.m. and on a 12-hour digital clock.			
I can read and interpret timetables and calendars.			
I can solve 'story' problems involving length, weight and capacity.			
I can explain and record how 'story' problems were solved.			
I can estimate answers to calculations and check my working.			
I can make up a 'story' problem for a measurement calculation.			

Unit 8 Number and problem solving

Can you remember?

a 1.2 cm = ☐ mm

b ☐ cm = 22 mm

c ☐ mm = 3.3 cm

d 49 mm = ☐ cm

e ☐ cm = 50 mm

f ☐ mm = 10 cm

Number patterns

  Circle all the odd numbers.

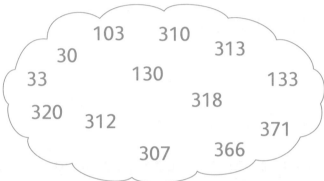

103 310
30 313
33 130 133
320 318
312 371
307 366

  Complete these counting sequences, then colour all the odd numbers.

Starting number					End number	Counting rule
200	197					−3
200	196					
199	202					
			199	203		
				294	304	
210					710	

44

Design your own number sequence that:

a has a pattern: odd, even, odd, even …

odd	even	odd	even	odd	even	odd	even	Counting rule
◯	◯	◯	◯	◯	◯	◯	◯	

b has a pattern: even, even, even … and would contain the number 100, but not 50.

even	even	even	even	even	even	even	even	Counting rule
◯	◯	◯	◯	◯	◯	◯	◯	

c has a pattern: odd, odd, odd, odd … and has the numbers 99 and 149 in it.

odd	odd	odd	odd	odd	odd	odd	odd	Counting rule
◯	◯	◯	◯	◯	◯	◯	◯	

 Play this game with a partner. Choose two numbers from the same cloud and find the total in the grid below. If your partner agrees on the answer, then colour it in your colour.

When you have used a number from a cloud, cross it out.

Odd numbers
11 13 15 17 19 21 23 25
27 29 31 33 35 37 39

Even numbers
12 14 16 18 22 24 26
28 32 34 36 38

Take it in turns. The winner is the first person to get a row of four numbers on the grid.

30	55	50	40	60	45
32	41	63	51	41	30
40	51	40	31	63	50
43	33	30	62	40	54
33	34	35	60	42	60
30	60	43	40	32	50

Multiplication and division

 Sort the calculations into the correct section of this Venn diagram.

18 × 4
20 × 5
50 × 5
52 × 5
52 × 3
13 × 7
91 × 6
91 × 7

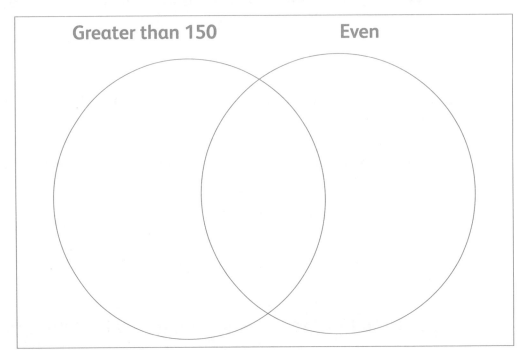

Greater than 150   **Even**

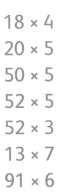 Write a story problem for each of these calculations.

Challenge your partner to sort the problems into order, from easiest (1) to hardest (4). Write 1 to 4 in the blocks.

4 × 4 = 16

4 × 7 = 28

4 × 10 = 40

36 ÷ 9 = 4

a Write your answers for the 9× table.

Colour the odd answers yellow. What do you notice?

b Now predict what will happen when you write the answers for the 6× table.

1 × 9 = ☐   6 × 9 = ☐   1 × 6 = ☐   6 × 6 = ☐

2 × 9 = ☐   7 × 9 = ☐   2 × 6 = ☐   7 × 6 = ☐

3 × 9 = ☐   8 × 9 = ☐   3 × 6 = ☐   8 × 6 = ☐

4 × 9 = ☐   9 × 9 = ☐   4 × 6 = ☐   9 × 6 = ☐

5 × 9 = ☐   10 × 9 = ☐   5 × 6 = ☐   10 × 6 = ☐

c Were you right? Complete these predictions about odd and even numbers.

• The 4× table will have ☐ even /odd ☐ numbers.

• The 3× table will have _____ .

Match the division to the correct remainder.

a 41 ÷ 3

b 51 ÷ 4

c 61 ÷ 5

d 71 ÷ 6

e 81 ÷ 7

f 91 ÷ 8

① ② ③ ④ ⑤

Work out the remainders for each of these divisions.

a 61 ÷ 3 = ⬭ remainder ⬭

b 61 ÷ 4 = ⬭ remainder ⬭

c 61 ÷ 5 = ⬭ remainder ⬭

d 61 ÷ 6 = ⬭ remainder ⬭

What do you notice?_____

Does this pattern carry on? Explain your answer.

_____

_____

 Compare 100 × 3 and 99 × 3.

100 × 3	99 × 3

Now compare 100 × 4 and 99 × 4.

100 × 4	99 × 4

How much more is 100 × 3 than 99 × 3?_____

What about 100 × 4 and 99 × 4?_____

Use what you notice to calculate:

99 × 8 = ⬚800⬚ – ⬭ = ⬭   99 × 5 = ⬭ – ⬭ = ⬭

99 × 2 = ⬭ – ⬭ = ⬭   99 × 9 = ⬭ – ⬭ = ⬭

Self-assessment

Unit 8 Number and problem solving

😊 I understand this well.

😐 I understand this, but I need more practice.

☹ I don't understand this.

I need more help with …

_____

_____

_____

Self-check statements	😊	😐	☹
I can say how to continue a number sequence, or how to work a sequence backwards.			
I can explain what the relationship is between pairs of numbers in a number sequence.			
I can say whether a number is odd or even.			
I can add or subtract multiples of 10, 100 or 1000.			
I know my 2×, 3×, 4×, 5×, 6×, 9× and 10× tables and can derive related division facts.			
I can double any number to 50, and double multiples of 10 and 100.			
I can multiply or divide a two-digit number by a single digit.			
I can state a related division calculation for a given multiplication and vice versa.			
I can check whether a statement is true by testing it with examples.			
I can make up a story problem to go with a multiplication or division.			
I can estimate the answer to multiplication and division calculations.			

Can you remember?

a $3 \times 14 = 30 + \boxed{} = 42$

b $5 \times 14 = 50 + \boxed{} = \boxed{}$

c $6 \times 14 = \boxed{} + \boxed{} = \boxed{}$

d $\boxed{} \times 15 = 20 + 10 = 30$

e $\boxed{} \times 15 = 50 + 25 = \boxed{}$

f $4 \times \boxed{} = 40 + 24 = \boxed{}$

Handling data

 1 Use a reading book. Choose a random page from the middle of the book. Count the letters in each word, then record the result in this tally chart.

Keep going until you have checked at least fifty words.

Word length	Tally	Total
One letter		
Two letters		
Three letters		
Four letters		
Five letters		
Six letters		
Seven letters		
More than seven letters		

2 Use the tally chart to create a bar chart of the results on the grid below.

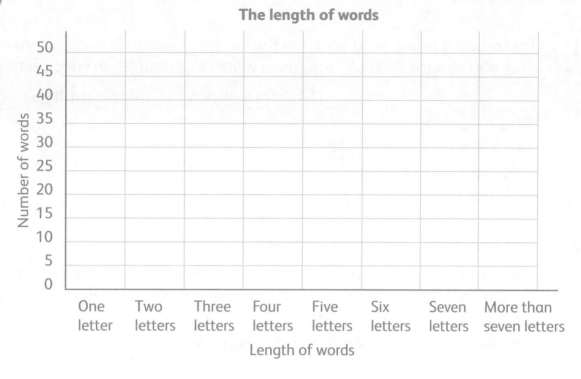

The length of words

3 Complete these sentences.

a The most common word length was _____.

b The least common word length was _____.

c The difference between the most and the least is _____.

d There were ⬜ more three-letter words than one-letter words.

e Write three questions of your own that you could ask about your chart.

_____

_____

_____

Problem solving

1 Try to add a number to each section of this Carroll diagram. If you think that you cannot fill a section, then write 'impossible' in that section.

	Multiple of ten	Not a multiple of ten
When doubled, the answer is a multiple of 10		
Does not double to a multiple of ten		

2 Add five numbers to each list below.

These numbers give a multiple of 3 when halved	These numbers leave a remainder when divided by two	These numbers give a multiple of 50 when doubled	These numbers give a multiple of 50 when halved

3 Use all the digits 1, 4, 6 and 8 to write as many odd numbers as you can. You can use each digit once only in each number that you write.

4 Explain why you could make more even numbers than odd numbers using these digits.

_____

_____

_____

Add a number to each section of this Venn diagram.

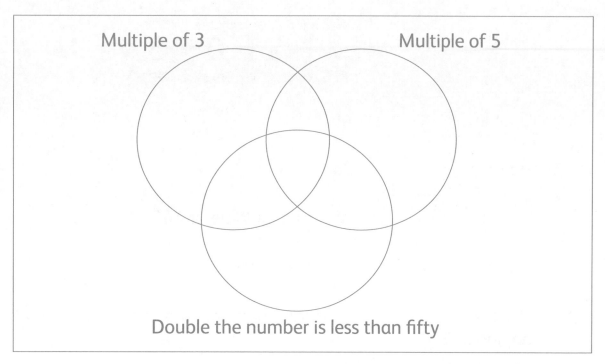

 Spin two 1–6 spinners and multiply the scores together. Place the results in this Venn diagram. Repeat four more times.

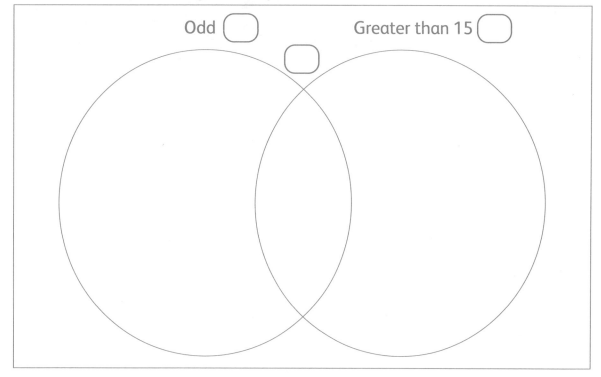

Put a tick (✓) in the section you predict will have the most numbers in when you have rolled 20 times. Now roll fifteen more times to see if you were correct.

7 Use these digits to complete these statements:

2   5   0   3

Double [ ][ ] is 46.

Half of [ ][ ] is 26.

[ ][ ][ ] doubles to a multiple of 100.

Half of [ ][ ][ ] is more than 100.

8 Use these digits to find different numbers that double to a number ending in 2.
Find six different solutions.

1   5   4   6

Double [ ]   is _____

Double [ ][ ]   is _____

Double [ ][ ]   is _____

Double [ ][ ]   is _____

Double [ ][ ][ ]   is _____

Double [ ][ ][ ]   is _____

Self-assessment

Unit 9 Handling data and problem solving

😊 I understand this well.

😐 I understand this, but I need more practice.

☹️ I don't understand this.

I need more help with …

_____

_____

_____

Self-check statements	😊	😐	☹️
I can read, write and use the vocabulary related to data.			
I can answer questions or solve a problem by interpreting graphs.			
I can sort objects and numbers using Venn or Carroll diagrams.			
I can use ordered lists and tables to help to solve problems systematically.			
I can explore statements and come to a decision about whether they are true or not.			
I can say whether a number is odd or even.			
I can double any number to 50, and double multiples of 10 and 100.			

Can you remember?

Write three numbers in each section of the Carroll diagram.

	Multiple of three	Not a multiple of three
Odd		
Even		

Numbers and the number system

1 Write the missing information.

a ⬚c = $1.25

b 152c = $⬚.⬚⬚

c 225c = $⬚.⬚⬚

d ⬚c = $2.20

e 202c = $⬚.⬚⬚

f ⬚c = $5.02

g ⬚c = $5.20

2 Write each answer using dollars and cents.

a 50c + 50c + 10c + 1c = $⬚.⬚⬚

b $1 + 50c + 25c = $⬚.⬚⬚

c $5 + 50c + 20c + 20c + 20c = $⬚.⬚⬚

d $10 + $1 + 10c + 1c = $⬚⬚.⬚⬚

e $10 + 10c = $⬚⬚.⬚⬚

f $10 + 1c = $⬚⬚.⬚⬚

Fractions and decimals

 1 Use the fraction wall to complete the missing information.

0.1	0.1	0.1	0.1	0.1	0.1	0.1	0.1	0.1	0.1
$\frac{1}{10}$	$\frac{1}{10}$	$\frac{1}{10}$	$\frac{1}{10}$	$\frac{1}{10}$	$\frac{1}{10}$	$\frac{1}{10}$	$\frac{1}{10}$	$\frac{1}{10}$	$\frac{1}{10}$

a $0.2 = \dfrac{\boxed{}}{10}$

b $0.8 = \dfrac{\boxed{}}{10}$

c $\boxed{}.\boxed{} = \dfrac{6}{10}$

d $\boxed{}.\boxed{} = \dfrac{9}{10}$

e $\dfrac{\boxed{}}{10} = 0.1$

f $\dfrac{3}{10} = \boxed{}.\boxed{}$

 2 Use this fraction wall to write the fractions as decimals.

0.1	0.1	0.1	0.1	0.1	0.1	0.1	0.1	0.1	0.1
$\frac{1}{10}$	$\frac{1}{10}$	$\frac{1}{10}$	$\frac{1}{10}$	$\frac{1}{10}$	$\frac{1}{10}$	$\frac{1}{10}$	$\frac{1}{10}$	$\frac{1}{10}$	$\frac{1}{10}$
$\frac{1}{5}$		$\frac{1}{5}$		$\frac{1}{5}$		$\frac{1}{5}$		$\frac{1}{5}$	

a $\frac{1}{5} = \boxed{}$ b $\frac{3}{5} = \boxed{}$ c $\frac{2}{5} = \boxed{}$ d $\frac{4}{5} = \boxed{}$ e $\frac{5}{5} = \boxed{}$

3 Insert **<**, **>** or **=** to make these statements correct.

a $\frac{1}{2} \boxed{} \frac{3}{5}$

b $\frac{1}{4} \boxed{} \frac{1}{5}$

c $\frac{1}{5} \boxed{} \frac{2}{10}$

d $\frac{2}{5} \boxed{} 0.4$

e $0.3 \boxed{} \frac{3}{5}$

f $\frac{1}{10} \boxed{} \frac{1}{100}$

Write each set of fractions in order on the number lines.
The first one has been done for you.

a

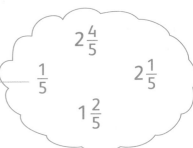

$2\frac{4}{5}$ $2\frac{1}{5}$ $\frac{1}{5}$ $1\frac{2}{5}$

b

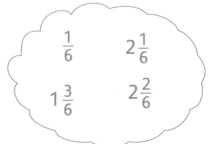

$\frac{1}{6}$ $2\frac{1}{6}$ $1\frac{3}{6}$ $2\frac{2}{6}$

c

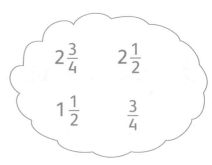

$2\frac{3}{4}$ $2\frac{1}{2}$ $1\frac{1}{2}$ $\frac{3}{4}$

 Write three fractions in each part of this Carroll diagram.

	Greater than $1\frac{1}{2}$	Less than $1\frac{1}{2}$
Denominator is odd		
Denominator is even		

Addition and subtraction

 Addition to 1. Use these diagrams to complete the calculations.

a $\frac{1}{5} +$ ⬚ $= 1$

b $\frac{2}{5} +$ ⬚ $= 1$

c ⬚ $+ \frac{2}{6} = 1$

d ⬚ $+ \frac{2}{7} = 1$

e $\frac{5}{8} + \frac{1}{8} +$ ⬚ $= 1$

f $\frac{2}{10} +$ ⬚ $+ \frac{5}{10} = 1$

 2

a Calculate $\frac{1}{5}$ of 80.

⬚ $\div$ ⬚ $=$ ⬚

b Calculate $\frac{1}{4}$ of 88.

⬚ $\div$ ⬚ $=$ ⬚

c Calculate $\frac{1}{3}$ of 87.

⬚ $\div$ ⬚ $=$ ⬚

d Calculate $\frac{1}{2}$ of 88.

⬚ $\div$ ⬚ $=$ ⬚

3 Explain why Alec is wrong, and shade the correct number of squares on the blank diagram.

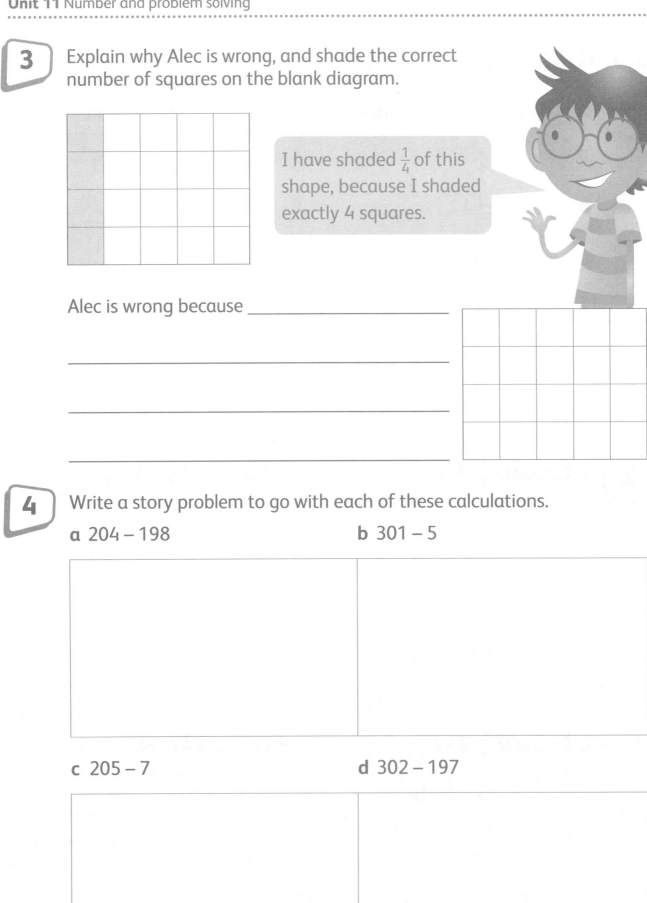

I have shaded $\frac{1}{4}$ of this shape, because I shaded exactly 4 squares.

Alec is wrong because _____

_____

_____

_____

4 Write a story problem to go with each of these calculations.

a 204 – 198

b 301 – 5

c 205 – 7

d 302 – 197

Self-assessment

Unit 11 Number and problem solving

😊	I understand this well.
😐	I understand this, but I need more practice.
🙁	I don't understand this.

I need more help with …

_____

_____

_____

Self-check statements	😊	😐	🙁
I can record money and measures using decimal notation.			
I can read and interpret negative numbers on a thermometer.			
I can identify simple equivalent fractions.			
I can express $\frac{1}{2}$ in several ways.			
I know the decimal equivalents of fractions.			
I can recognise and order fractions and mixed numbers.			
I can link fractions to division situations.			
I can find simple fractions of quantities.			
I can add pairs of fractions that make 1.			
I can add, subtract and find the difference between near multiples of ten.			
I can subtract a small number from a number just bigger than 100, or a multiple of 100.			

Can you remember?

a $\frac{1}{3}$ of 24 is ☐

b $\frac{1}{4}$ of 12 is ☐

c $\frac{1}{6}$ of 12 is ☐

d $\frac{1}{3}$ of ☐ is 12

The metric system

1 Show the level of the water after half a litre has been added to each.

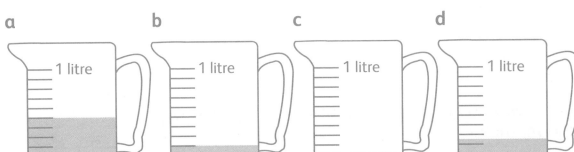

a   **b**   **c**   **d**

e

f

g

h

2 Complete the missing information.

a [ ] + 100 ml + 50 ml = 1ℓ

b 200 ml + [ ] + 50 ml = 1ℓ

c 125 ml + 125 ml + [ ] = 1ℓ

d 125 ml + [ ] + 125 ml = 2ℓ

e 350 ml + 100 ml + [ ] = 1ℓ

f [ ] + 350 ml + [ ] = $1\frac{1}{2}$ℓ

3 The glass has a capacity of 250 ml.
How many glasses would it take to fill each of the containers?

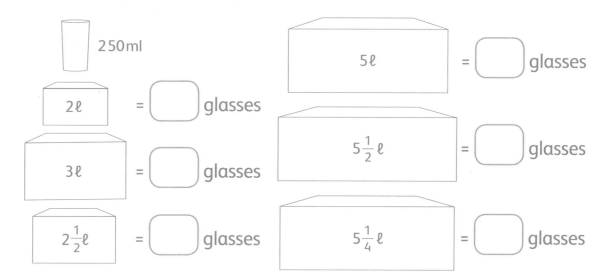

250 ml

2ℓ = [ ] glasses

3ℓ = [ ] glasses

$2\frac{1}{2}$ℓ = [ ] glasses

5ℓ = [ ] glasses

$5\frac{1}{2}$ℓ = [ ] glasses

$5\frac{1}{4}$ℓ = [ ] glasses

10ℓ = [ ] glasses

12ℓ = [ ] glasses

Length, area and perimeter

 Add to each shape so that it has an area of 10 squares.

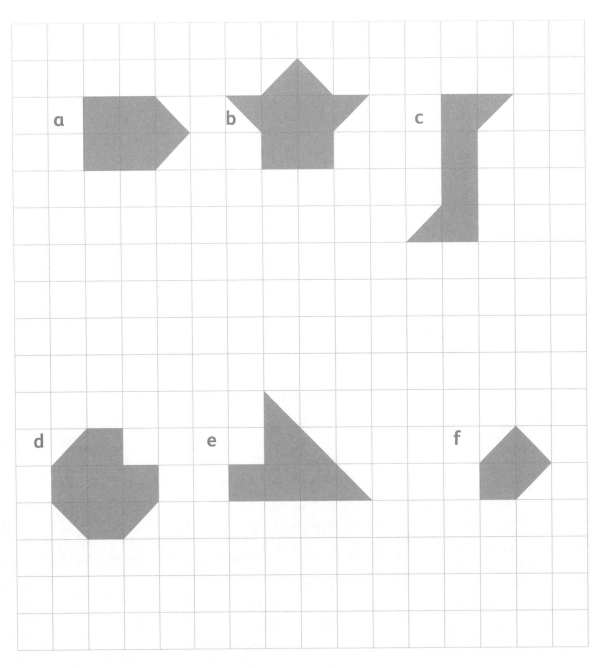

2 Follow the instructions to approximate the area of the shape below.

a Shade all the whole squares, and count them.

I counted ⬜ whole squares.

b Shade pairs of half-squares.

The half-squares are equal to ⬜ whole squares.

c Find other parts of squares that would join together to make a whole square.

These are approximately equal to ⬜ whole squares.

d Combine these ideas to make a final approximation.

My approximation is ⬜ squares for the area of the whole shape.

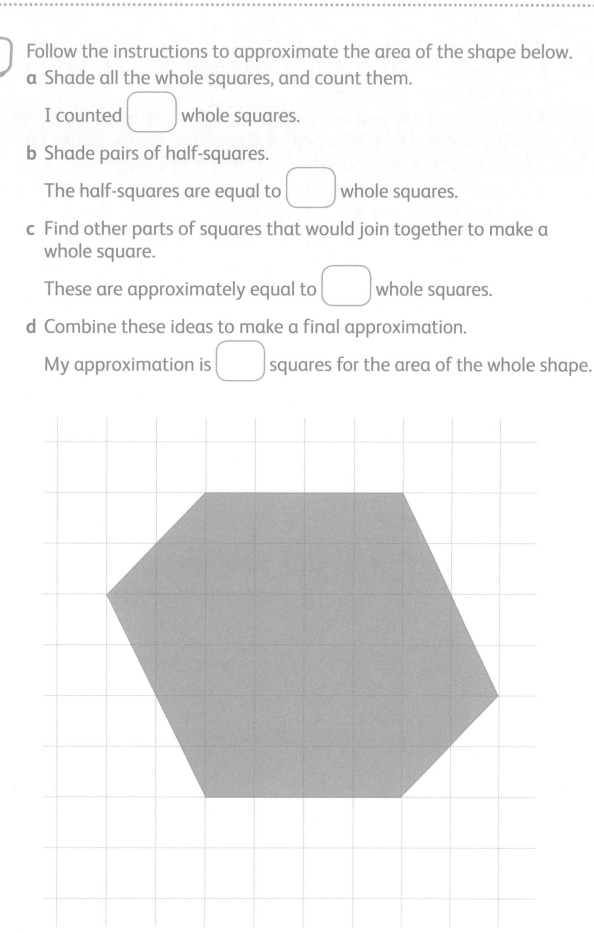

3 Here is a game to play with a partner. Each choose a colour.

Spin a 1–6 spinner. This tells you how many half-squares to shade in one of the polygons below.

You can only shade into one polygon at a time. That means, if you spin 3, you can shade three half-squares in one of the shapes, but you cannot split your shading between two different shapes.

If you complete one of the polygons, you get points equal to the area of the shape you completed. Keep a tally.

At the end, count who has scored the most points.

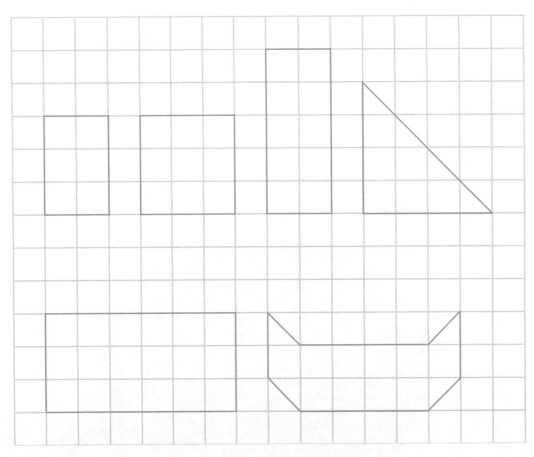

Player name	Tally	Total
Player 1:		
Player 2:		

Time

September						
Sun	Mon	Tues	Wed	Thurs	Fri	Sat
			14	15	16	17
18	19	20				

1 Before you complete the calendar, predict how many of each day there will be in this month.

I predict ☐ Mondays.   I predict ☐ Fridays.

I predict ☐ Tuesdays.   I predict ☐ Saturdays.

I predict ☐ Wednesdays.   I predict ☐ Sundays.

I predict ☐ Thursdays.

2 Now complete the calendar to see if your predictions were correct.

3 Add these events to the calendar by reading the clues. You may write them in, or draw a picture for each one.

- Orlando's party is on the last Saturday of the month.
- Lia's party is on the first Tuesday of the month.
- The school play is two weeks after the 4th September.
- The disco is exactly one week before the 2nd October.
- The school holiday starts on 29th August, and lasts for five days.

Self-assessment

Unit 12 Measures and problem solving

😊 I understand this well.

😐 I understand this, but I need more practice.

☹️ I don't understand this.

I need more help with …

_____

_____

_____

Self-check statements	😊	😐	☹️
I can measure lengths, weights or capacity in different units and record my results.			
I can use the metric units for length, mass and capacity.			
I can interpret and read measuring scales.			
I can draw rectangles and measure and calculate their perimeters.			
I can use squares to find the areas of simple shapes.			
I can use a square grid to find the areas of simple shapes.			
I can read simple timetables and use a calendar.			
I can solve 'story' problems involving length, weight and capacity.			
I can explain and record how 'story' problems were solved.			
I can explain my reasoning orally, and in writing, and test whether it is correct.			

Unit 13 Number and problem solving

Can you remember?

Write the digital time for each clock.

a [   ] . [   ] [   ]   (a.m.)

b [   ] [   ] . [   ] [   ]   (p.m.)

c [   ] . [   ] [   ]   (a.m.)

d [   ] [   ] . [   ] [   ]   (p.m.)

e [   ] . [   ] [   ]   (a.m.)

f [   ] [   ] . [   ] [   ]   (p.m.)

Number patterns

1   Write the missing numbers in these sequences.

a

110	130	150					250

Rule: add [20]

b

350	330	310					210

Rule: subtract [   ]

c

515		555		595			

Rule: [   ]

d

99		109		119			

Rule: [   ]

e

999		899				699	

Rule: [   ]

f

101		305		509			

Rule: [   ]

2   Add these numbers to the correct part of the Carroll diagrams.

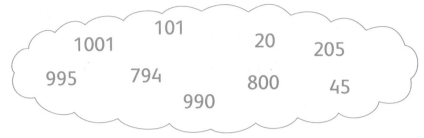

a

	Odd	Even
Multiple of five		
Not a multiple of five		

b

	Multiple of ten	Not a multiple of ten
Multiple of a hundred		
Not a multiple of a hundred		

c

	Multiple of ten	Not a multiple of ten
Multiple of five		
Not a multiple of five		

Multiplication and division

1 Complete the missing numbers.

a
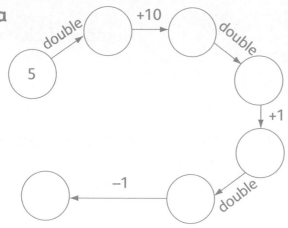

b
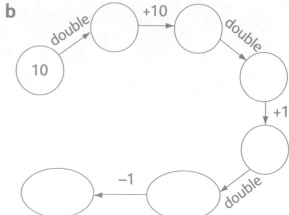

c
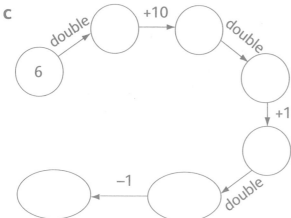

d
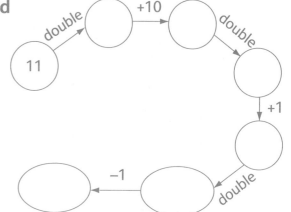

2 Colour these grids based on the instructions.

a Two red for every three blue

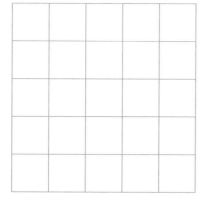

Number of red =

Number of blue =

b Three red for every two blue

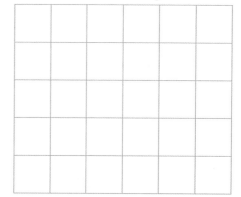

Number of red =

Number of blue =

c Two red for every four blue

Number of red = ☐

Number of blue = ☐

d Two red for every three blue

Number of red = ☐

Number of blue = ☐

3 Some of these divisions are wrong. Write a multiplication to match each division.

Solve the multiplication to see which divisions were correct.

a 36 ÷ 6 = 5 6 × 5 = ☐	b 72 ÷ 3 = 14	c 72 ÷ 6 = 12
d 96 ÷ 3 = 32	e 96 ÷ 6 = 15	f 84 ÷ 6 = 14

4 Which offer is the cheapest if you need to buy 100 pens?
Draw a diagram to explain your calculations for each offer.

Offer A: 4 pens for $3	Offer B: 5 pens for $2.50
Offer C: 10 pens for $7	Offer D: 20 pens for $12

Offer _____ is the cheapest to buy 100 pens.

Unit 13 Number and problem solving

😊 I understand this well.

😐 I understand this, but I need more practice.

☹ I don't understand this.

I need more help with …

_____

_____

_____

Self-check statements	😊	😐	☹
I can say whether a number up to 1000 is a multiple of 5, 10, or 100.			
I can say how to continue a number sequence forwards or backwards.			
I can explain the relationship between pairs of numbers in a number sequence.			
I can say whether a number is odd or even.			
I can find and explain patterns when adding pairs of odd or even numbers.			
I can add or subtract multiples of 10, 100 or 1000.			
I can state a related division calculation for a given multiplication and vice versa.			
I can estimate the answer to multiplication and division calculations.			
I can predict whether or not my answer is greater or less than the actual answer.			
I can explain why I think a method may be the best for a given calculation.			
I can explain the methods I use orally, or in writing.			
I can check whether a statement is true by testing it with examples.			

Unit 14 Geometry and problem solving

Can you remember?

a 11 × ☐ = 88

b ☐ × 11 = 22

c 22 × 4 = ☐

d 31 × 4 = ☐

e 42 × 4 = ☐

f 53 × 5 = ☐

Classifying shapes

 Complete the drawings of these prisms. Write the number of vertices, faces and edges for each shape.

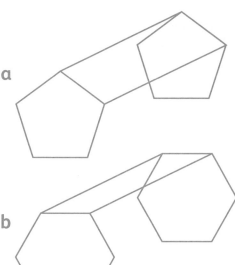

a

Number of vertices = ☐

Number of edges = ☐

Number of faces = ☐

b

Number of vertices = ☐

Number of edges = ☐

Number of faces = ☐

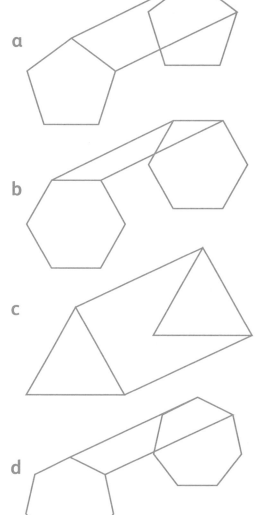

c

Number of vertices = ☐

Number of edges = ☐

Number of faces = ☐

d

Number of vertices = ☐

Number of edges = ☐

Number of faces = ☐

2 Follow the instructions to draw each shape.

Challenge 1: Draw a four-sided shape with zero right angles.

Challenge 2: Draw a triangle with one right angle.

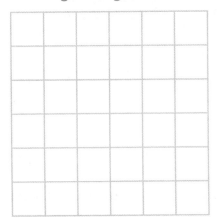

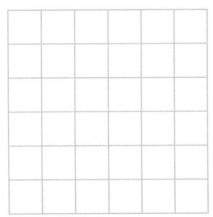

Challenge 3: Draw a pentagon with zero right angles.

Challenge 4: Draw a hexagon with two right angles.

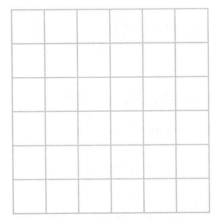

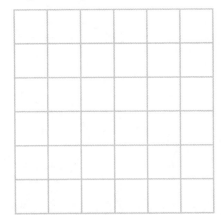

Challenge 5: Draw a heptagon with an odd number of right angles.

Challenge 6: Draw a different heptagon with an odd number of right angles.

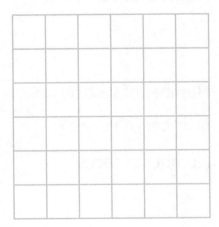

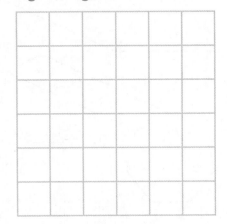

3-D and 2-D shapes

 Draw lines of symmetry on these shapes. Three of the shapes have two lines of symmetry. One shape has no lines of symmetry.

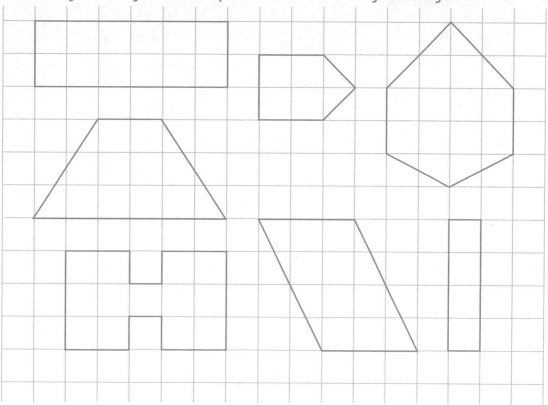

 Draw six different nets of a cube. Compare them with your partner's. Each score a point for a net that is not on your partner's grid. Then use construction materials to check that each one does make a cube.

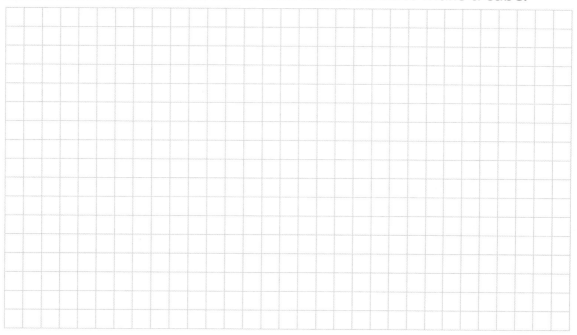

Position and movement

Mark all the acute angles with an A, and all the obtuse angles with an O on these shapes.

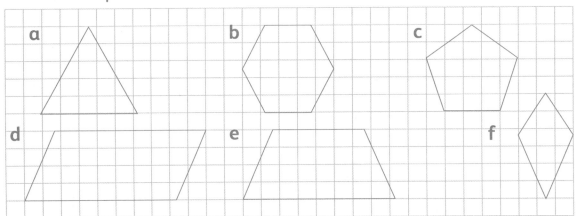

a   b   c
d   e   f

2 Look at these turns.

quarter-turn   half-turn   three quarter-turn   whole-turn

Find a different solution for each statement below. The first one has been done for you.

a [a half-turn + a quarter-turn] $= \frac{3}{4}$ turn

[ ] $= \frac{3}{4}$ turn

b [ ] = whole turn

[ ] = whole turn

[ ] = whole turn

c [ ] $= 1\frac{1}{2}$ turns

[ ] $= 1\frac{1}{2}$ turns

[ ] $= 1\frac{1}{2}$ turns

[ ] $= 1\frac{1}{2}$ turns

3 Write the grid references for each of the circles.

a ◯ b ◯ c ◯ d ◯

4 Write directions for the triangle to travel to the star, and collect all the circles on the way. You cannot travel through the shaded squares. Include the number of squares and the compass directions, for example: 3 East.

_____

_____

_____

_____

_____

_____

Self-assessment

Unit 14 Geometry and problem solving

😀 I understand this well.

😐 I understand this, but I need more practice.

☹ I don't understand this.

I need more help with …

_____

_____

_____

Self-check statements	😀	😐	☹
I can name, describe and draw 2-D and 3-D shapes.			
I can explore statements and come to a decision about whether they are true or not.			
I can make nets of simple 3-D shapes and rearrange these to make new nets.			
I can find and sketch lines of symmetry in 2-D shapes and patterns.			
I can identify shapes and symmetry in drawings and around me.			
I can use a square grid to identify the position of things.			
I know that a right angle, quarter-turn and 90° are equivalent.			
I can give directions to follow a path.			